DATE DUE

MAR 3 '95			

#47-0103 Pre-Gummed

EDWARD R. MURROW

by Sprague Vonier

For a free color catalog describing Gareth Stevens' list of high-quality children's books call 1-800-433-0942

Picture Credits
© John Caucalosi/Tom Stack and Associates, 13 (bottom); CBS Photography, 4, 28, 54, 55 (top); © Curt Teich Postcard Collection, 1989, 12, 19 (top and bottom), 24; Courtesy of the Edwin Ginn Library, Tufts University, 43, 45; Flag Research Center, 50; © Gareth Stevens, 1989/Courtesy of Art Lange Collection, 22, 42/Courtesy of the Moshe ben Shimon Collection, 55 (bottom); © Bob McKeever/Tom Stack and Associates, 1981, 17; © Harry Quinn, 1989, cover; © John Shaw/Tom Stack and Associates, 7; © Tom Stack/Tom Stack and Associates, 44 (left); © Spencer Swanger/Tom Stack and Associates, 14; UPI/ Bettman Newsphotos, 21, 27, 30, 31, 32, 34, 35, 36, 39, 41, 46, 51, 57; Washington State University Libraries, Historical Photograph Collection, 8 (Neg. #83-138), 10 (Neg. #89-265), 13 (top) (Neg. #89-264), 15 (Neg. #70-012), 16 (Neg. #88-335), 23 (Neg. #83-139), 37 (Neg. #83-114), 44 (top) (Neg. #79-132), 48 (Neg. #83-148), 56 (Neg. #83-134), 59 (Neg. #79-133). The reproduction rights to all photographs and illustrations in this book are controlled by the individuals or institutions credited above and may not be reproduced without their permission.

A Gareth Stevens Children's Books edition

Edited, designed, and produced by
Gareth Stevens Children's Books
1555 North RiverCenter Drive
Milwaukee, WI 53212, USA

Library of Congress Cataloging-in-Publication Data

Vonier, Sprague.
    Edward R. Murrow / by Sprague Vonier.
       p. cm. — (People who have helped the world)
    Summary: Follows the career of the foreign correspondent whose radio news broadcasts during World War II made history and enabled him to expand into television journalism.
    Includes index.
    ISBN 0-8368-0100-8
    1. Murrow, Edward R.—Juvenile literature. 2. Journalists—United States—Biography—Juvenile literature. [1. Murrow, Edward R. 2. Journalists.] I. Title. II. Series.
PN4874.M89V66 1989   070'.92'4—dc19 [B]   [92]   89-4344

C 921
MUR

Series conceived by Helen Exley
Series editor: Rhoda Irene Sherwood
Editor: Valerie Weber
Editorial assistant: Scott Enk
Picture research: Matthew Groshek
Layout: Kristi Ludwig

Printed in the United States of America

1 2 3 4 5 6 7 8 9 95 94 93 92 91 90 89

EDWARD R. MURROW

His courage and ideals set the standard for broadcast journalism

by Sprague Vonier

Gareth Stevens Children's Books
MILWAUKEE

Man on the rooftop

You are standing on a London rooftop in the dead of night. Overhead you hear waves of German bombers, unseen except when caught in a searchlight. The sky is filled with barrage balloons, their bellies lit by anti-aircraft bursts. The air smells of fire. On the ground, bombs explode on all sides. Fires spread like running water through houses, factories, and office buildings.

In your hand, you hold a microphone. You ignore danger and describe everything you see. No matter what happens, you keep talking:

"Straightaway in front of me the searchlights are working. I can see one or two bursts of antiaircraft fire. . . . On the roof across the way I can see a man wearing a tin hat, with a pair of powerful night glasses to his eyes, scanning the sky."

Millions listen

Three thousand miles away, across the Atlantic Ocean, radios all over the United States are tuned to the reporter. Housewives and factory workers, schoolchildren and farmers, senators and dogcatchers stop their lives to hear you. Even the president listens.

Your voice is so strong and clear that fifty years later, people who listened then will say they can still hear it in their imagination. You will help your fellow citizens understand the terrible war that will soon engulf them too. Your words will influence political leaders around the world. You become the most famous reporter of your day. It will be said you "set standards of excellence that remain unsurpassed." Today, journalism students still listen to your tapes, read your scripts, and study your TV programs.

Your name is Edward R. Murrow — a name you have given to yourself — and a long, winding, and unexpected road brings you to this rooftop.

Opposite: Edward R. Murrow as he appeared in 1953, near the height of his career as a radio and television news reporter.

"Murrow gets brighter every year because he stands out like the burning star that never leaves the sky."

Joe Wershba,
CBS reporter-producer

5

The voice of history

Edward R. Murrow is sometimes called "the voice of history." He was not only the most famous news reporter of his time but the most honored of all times. He won five Peabody awards, the highest broadcasters' award, and every other award worth having.

He did more than five thousand radio and television news broadcasts, some of which influenced the course of history, and he headed the United States Information Agency in a time of great trouble. But more than all this, he gave voice to the hopes, fears, and troubles of humanity.

The unexpected road started a long way from big cities and the conveniences of the twentieth century.

Loud voice in the woods

It was time for the new baby to be born in the Murrow household. A young uncle was sent to fetch the doctor, but it was a long hike and the doctor didn't get there until four o'clock in the morning. Baby Murrow had already arrived.

Legend has it that his uncle and the doctor could hear him from a mile away. They couldn't know, of course, that his voice some day would carry around the world. Even the name of his birthplace — Polecat Creek, North Carolina — told you it was in the backwoods. The house had no electricity, no plumbing, no running water and, of course, no telephone. It was heated by a huge fireplace in the main room, where all the cooking was done. Each night, the fireplace provided the light for reading a chapter of the Bible.

The history of the Murrow family in the United States went back to a time before the American Revolution. They were Quakers and had settled in Center Community of Friends, Guilford County, the colony around Polecat Creek, more than one hundred years before Baby Murrow's birth. They were against slavery and against the Civil War, a dangerous position for people living in the South. After the war, Murrow's grandfather was a leader in the work of the Reconstruction, which included trying to help former slaves.

The family of Murrow's mother had fought for the Confederacy. Her father, George Van Buren Lamb, was a captain in the 22nd North Carolina Regiment.

The hill country of North Carolina today looks much the same as it did when Egbert Murrow was born. Large, closely knit families settled together in small communities and depended on each other for help and spiritual support. It was a big step to break away from these sheltering hills, as Ed's family did.

Egbert Roscoe

English, Irish, Scottish, German and, it was said, even a little Cherokee blood flowed through the infant's veins. This new baby seemed to spring from the very soul of the nation's character, from its sorrows and its strengths: the Civil War, the hard life on the land, the moving on to the frontier, the struggle for education, the search for prosperity.

Baby Murrow was named Egbert Roscoe Murrow when he started out in life, a name he didn't like when he grew a little older. He had two brothers, Dewey, two, and Lacey, four. As the youngest, he was always hustling to keep up, tagging along and demanding to do everything his older brothers could do.

Perhaps it was his childhood need to catch up that gave him his lifelong drive and ambition and a voice that commanded attention. Relatives would recall the strangeness of that oddly mature voice coming from the small boy's body. You can almost hear him hollering, "Wait for me!"

His brothers made fun of him and his big voice, calling him "the Egg" and "Eber Blowhard." The nicknames stuck and, later, followed him to school. No wonder he wanted to change his name!

The engaging smile and the level, penetrating gaze that became familiar to millions and helped Murrow become a superb reporter seem already in place in this baby picture. Also evident is his air of concentrated attention. Nothing seems to escape this boy.

Radio is born, too

It's hard to imagine how different from today's was the world Egbert Murrow was born into on April 25, 1908. The twentieth century and many of the things we take for granted were just getting started. New inventions seemed to crowd on stage every day.

Human speech had been sent by radio for the first time only a few years earlier. In New York City just a year before, Lee De Forest had set up history's first regularly scheduled radio station. The year Egbert was born, De Forest made a historic first broadcast from the Eiffel Tower in Paris and drew worldwide attention to radio.

The first Ford Model T automobiles were rolling off the assembly line then, but Egbert would be five years old before he would see a car.

Events and personalities that would be important during Murrow's life were also moving onto the stage. Lyndon B. Johnson was born that year. So was Joseph R. McCarthy. The paths of these three men, Johnson, McCarthy, and Murrow, born hundreds of miles apart, would cross several times.

There were only forty-six states in the Union when Egbert was born (years later, he would play a small part in the making of two new states). The U.S. population was ninety million souls, barely a third of what it is today.

The year Egbert turned one, 1909, marked the first flight across the English Channel. And the next year, the first newsreel was shown.

None of this may have mattered to the people of Polecat Creek, but Egbert wouldn't have to wait long to meet the great outside world.

Everyone worked

Perhaps the Murrows were poor by some standards but, Ed Murrow later joked, "We didn't know it." Everyone had to work to keep things going. By the time little Egbert was four years old, he was hauling water from the outside pump, bringing in firewood for cooking, feeding pigs, and scattering grain to the chickens. He learned early in life to work hard.

It was a strict household. Mother Ethel Murrow didn't allow any smoking, drinking, card playing, or coarse talk, and she insisted that the Bible be read every evening and more than once on Sunday. She spoke much the same way her Bible was written, in the old English way that had been kept alive in these isolated back hills for many years.

The boys' father, Roscoe, was easygoing and cheerful, although he didn't talk much. He was also an expert outdoorsman, and he taught his sons the arts of hunting, fishing, and woodcraft.

Grandfather Lamb, "the Captain," was a great storyteller. In those days, storytelling was one of the few entertainments available to people, so the boys liked to slip through the woods about a half mile to the Captain's house and hear him tell about his days in the Confederate army, about Indians, and about clever old horse traders.

Little by little, even in early childhood, the qualities that Ed Murrow would use to become famous began to take shape: the richness of his language, his ear for a good story, his determination, and his feelings for humanity.

Call of the West

In those times, the West had a strong pull on poor Southerners. Farming was hard and much of the South was in the grip of a depression. And as Quakers who believed that the body was a temple that should not be defiled with smoke, the Murrows refused to raise tobacco, the only crop that promised to bring in a little cash.

Ethel Murrow's cousins, the Cobles, had moved west some years before and were doing well farming in Washington State. They urged the young Murrow family to join them.

So the Murrows sold everything — the year's crop, the farm, the mule team, even the furniture — and prepared to leave the home place where the two families had settled so long before. They packed their clothes, a few household items, some keepsakes, and food for the long train journey.

Their destination was Skagit County, Washington, near the Puget Sound, almost all the way to the Pacific Ocean. They couldn't have gone much farther and stayed in the United States.

Ed Murrow's parents, Ethel and Roscoe, lived on the edge of poverty much of their lives but clung to an image that would mark them as respectable, average U.S. citizens. Ethel laid down strict rules, based on her religious beliefs, against smoking, drinking, dancing, and the use of bad language. Even Roscoe had to go outside to light up his pipe.

Clear across the country

It was a long journey by train. They sat up six days and six nights. Ethel Murrow strictly rationed the food she'd brought along. Every nickel had to be saved for essentials. The year was 1913. Egbert was five years old, Dewey was seven, and Lacey was nine. It must have been a wild train ride with three young boys cooped up day and night.

The place they came to, Blanchard, Washington, where the Cobles lived, was little more than a frontier town — wood-frame stores and houses, mud streets, wooden sidewalks, a two-room school, and three hundred people. But it was a boom town for the logging industry. So there was a housing shortage and everything was expensive. The small amount of money that remained from selling all they owned was not enough to pay for a roof over their heads.

Life in a logging town

They pitched a tent on an unused part of the Cobles' farm, low-lying wetland that often flooded, leaving the floor of the tent awash. Although Roscoe Murrow was strong and a good worker, he had a hard time finding and keeping a job.

Their money dwindled. Things got so bad that all their lives, the boys remembered nights when they got barely enough to eat, and they knew that their parents went hungry. They were too proud to take charity. But Ethel was a strong-willed woman and she refused to give up. It was she who kept them going.

Then things took a turn for the better. Roscoe landed a job with a logging company working on the railroad that hauled logs down from the lumber camps. He liked the work and soon became a locomotive engineer, one of the better jobs. The family had enough for the necessities now but not much more.

Since there were not enough Quakers to support a meetinghouse, Ethel joined the Methodist church and soon was an influence in the community. From her boys she continued to demand obedience and achievement. They did well in school. Whenever there were odd jobs around the neighborhood, she saw that her boys were the ones to get them.

Their mother rarely made any outward show of affection but her constant concern for their welfare carried its own message of her love. She still required them to take turns reading from the Bible every night and instilled in them a strong sense of right and wrong. As the youngest in the family, Egbert was neither babied nor bullied. He held his own.

Life wasn't all chores and discipline, though. The boys loved to roughhouse with their father, threatening to turn the house upside-down when he came home from work. They fished in the wild rivers and streams and, when they were old enough, hunted in woods that in those days were filled with game.

All-around boy

When it was time to go to high school, Egbert followed his brothers to the little town of Edison, named after Thomas Edison, who had helped bring electricity to much of the nation. Edison High had only about fifty students and five teachers.

Egbert's brother, Dewey, was still at Edison, but Lacey had gone on to Washington State College. Both Lacey and Dewey were leaders in school activities. They were members of the school orchestra, played on the baseball team, and sang in the glee club.

Work in the lumber camps was hard and dangerous. Most of it was done with the muscle power of men and animals. Even as a teenager, Murrow was able to hold his own with the rough, strong men with whom he worked. He started at the bottom of the business as an axman.

Now Egbert also played on the baseball and basketball teams, played the ukulele in the school orchestra, and won roles in the student operettas. But his greatest satisfaction came as a member of the debating team. He found that he had a talent for it.

He may also have glimpsed some of the great issues he would grapple with in a few years when he and his teammates won the regional championship. They answered "yes" to the question, "Resolved: The United States Should Enter the World Court."

Egbert was also known as a debater outside of school. Neither the subject nor the side he argued mattered to him. In fact, he spoke so well on these occasions that a neighbor on a nearby farm asked him to preach at his funeral.

He led a busy life. There were always the chores to do at home, of course. Plus he tried to earn money doing other work. Early mornings and after school he drove the school bus, a job he had inherited from Dewey. And there were odd jobs in the neighborhood, usually working for some farmer who had often been promised help by his mother.

The old Murrow luck

One such occasion symbolized what Egbert came to call the "old Murrow luck." He planned to go hunting but found that his services had been promised to a neighboring farmer. Disappointed, he carried his shotgun with him to his job. He worked until almost sundown. When he cut through the fields on the way home, he bagged two birds. Once home, he found that his brother had hunted all afternoon and shot nothing.

Hunting and fishing were not only sources of great pleasure throughout his life; during his boyhood and youth, they helped put food on the table. When he sold a rabbit or a duck, hunting was also a way to earn a few cents. So it was not surprising that he would associate a good day's catch with good luck. But few people worked harder at making their own luck.

The storytellers

During the summers, starting when he was fourteen years old, Egbert worked in the logging camps. The tradition of storytelling in the bunkhouses and around the campfires at night continued to tune his ear to the language and to teach him the power of the human voice. He listened carefully and watched the way men reacted as a story unfolded. Occasionally, he tried his own hand at storytelling, sometimes using the well-polished tales his Grandfather Lamb told so well.

When Murrow returned to school as a senior, he became both class president and the president of the entire student body. He was already known as a talented speaker. The yearbook mentions his "gift of elocution," and he was named "the boy who had done most for the school."

In the woods

The young man had hoped to go to the University of Virginia to study history, but money was still scarce. So he decided to work in the lumber camps for a full year to make money for college.

This time he went to the virgin forests of the Olympic Peninsula, where new logging operations were being opened up. Previous to this, only Indians had been in many parts of these woods.

Below: Ed Murrow smiles for his high school portrait.

Bottom: In 1925, the Murrow family moved to Beaver, Washington, in the shadow of the Olympic mountain range.

Much of rural Washington State was still pristine frontier country when the Murrow boys were growing up. For the rest of his life, Ed Murrow would talk longingly of the time he spent in the woods, hunting, fishing, and later logging. He liked to describe himself as a poor boy from the woods and farm at heart.

He had grown into a tall, strong youth who seemed older than his seventeen years — except when he broke into an appealing grin. Egbert became Ed, an easier name to live with among lumberjacks.

His willingness to work and quick mind caught the eye of the logging company's chief "lumber cruiser," whose job it was to go into the uncharted forest and map it for cutting. The lumber cruiser chose Ed to be his assistant and compass man. Alone they ranged into the forest, ahead of the work crews. They slept in the open under a sky that was as yet undimmed by lights from the cities or by smoke from the factories.

A lonely life

This part of Washington State was among the most beautiful places in the world, with towering Mount Olympus always in view. The stately fir and pine trees were hundreds of years old, some of them rising three hundred feet (90 m). The streams were fresh, the lakes were clear and deep, and both abounded in fish.

Far from human settlement, this life was often lonely but young Ed thrived on it. Marking out lumber reserves and bedding down alone in the wilderness gave him plenty of chances to think about life and to learn to rely on himself. But Ed Murrow wanted to go to college. With a year's pay, less some money he gave to his parents, he headed for Pullman, Washington, and Washington State College.

A new name

The year was 1926. The NBC radio network, which would grow into a broadcasting giant, had just gone on the air. Hirohito became emperor of Japan. And the girl child who would become Queen Elizabeth II was born. All of these events would become important to Murrow, but the most important thing to him at the time was college.

Murrow felt he should do something permanent about his name. He'd been called "Ed" in the lumber camps, but now he could take his new name all the time. He called himself Edward R. Murrow, the name under which he would become world-famous. It seemed to fit his personality, which bloomed in the excitement of the college campus.

Washington State College was what was usually called a "cow college," the sort of school founded to help educate the farming population. Both of Ed's brothers had gone there before him — and left their marks, as they always did. Lacey had done well and gone on to win a place in the state highway department. Dewey had dropped out after his second year and gone to South America to hunt emeralds.

For Ed there was the usual problem of money. He had to hold down two jobs, one washing dishes for meals and another doing maintenance in a girls' dormitory in exchange for a room in the basement. His brother Lacey decided to help out financially.

When Ed enrolled, Washington State College dominated the small town of Pullman. Its enrollment of 2,800 students nearly matched in number the town's 3,000 residents. The college's principal purpose was to teach agriculture, mining, and engineering — the practical crafts badly needed in the developing Northwest.

Early radio station

Both of his brothers had been popular members of Kappa Sigma, so Ed was eagerly welcomed into that fraternity house. He also continued to work a couple of part-time jobs just to make ends meet, including brute jobs hauling bags of wheat in the railroad yards on the weekends.

But the "old Murrow luck" seemed to be working. Washington State College was one of the first colleges in the nation to have its own radio station. It was operated as part of the speech department and gave Ed Murrow his first taste of broadcasting.

It was unlikely that he dreamed of becoming a broadcast news journalist, however, for there would be no such profession until Ed helped to develop it years later.

His natural talents and his memory of success as a high school debater made him want to switch to the speech department.

An inspired teacher

He found an inspired teacher — or perhaps she found him — who saw promise in this gangling youth with the big ears and the broad smile. Her name was Ida Lou Anderson and she taught advanced speech.

A childhood attack of polio left her with a double curvature of the spine. She was barely five feet (1.5 m) tall and in almost constant pain. But she loved acting and public speaking and would not allow her disability to stand in her way. In college, she starred in several plays and won every speaking contest in the state.

Anderson was the kind of teacher who filled her students with enthusiasm. They loved to crowd around her after class and walk home with her. Her house was often full of students discussing plays, reading poetry, or just having fun talking. But her favorite student was Ed Murrow, and she began to teach him not only how to use his voice but also a love of the English language and of ideas.

Murrow always knew that to succeed, we need the help of others. Throughout his life, just as he had when he worked in the forest as a lumberjack, he turned to those who could help him.

In the same way, Murrow helped other people. He was able to spot talent and character, and in later years, almost all of the reporters and correspondents he hired became stars in their own right. Once he decided to hire someone, he gave that person all the help he possibly could.

Ida Lou Anderson sought the best in her students and worked with each one to develop their talents to the fullest. She set them in competition, not with each other, but with themselves.

"[Ida Lou Anderson] taught me one must have more than a good bluff to really live."
Edward R. Murrow

The Meditations

Assisting others may have been one of the many lessons he learned from Ida Lou Anderson. In Murrow, she had an eager pupil. To polish Ed's writing and to give it power and rhythm, she introduced him to the great poets, especially to the works of Shakespeare.

She also placed in his hands a book that seems to say just what he believed, that gave expression to the creed of hard work and honesty. It was the *Meditations* of Marcus Aurelius Antoninus, a Roman emperor who had set down his philosophy of life in a short book of brief sayings. Murrow studied these, committed many to memory, and liked to quote them:

"Dig down into yourself, where the source of goodness is ever ready to gush forth, if you always dig deeply."
"Do not feel shame at being helped."
"If you perform the task before you and follow the right rule of reason steadfastly . . . preserve the spirit within you in its pure state . . . truthful in every word you utter, you will lead the good life."

Although these words were the words of an emperor-philosopher, they could have been those of his mother reminding him to "hoe to the end of the row." Perhaps these words also gave shape to his own thoughts when he was alone in the woods.

Anderson spent many extra hours with Murrow, having him read the classics aloud, coaching him on the best way to speak the words and talking about how writers use language to express powerful ideas. She was determined to make Murrow her masterpiece.

A brush with death

Each summer he returned to the woods to work as an assistant timber cruiser. One year in the lumber camps, he was caught in a forest fire and nearly lost his life. It is possible that the smoke and superheated air damaged his lungs, but he was not given any medical treatment. In those days, it was all part of the danger of working in the logging camps. He was also a heavy user of cigarettes. The combination might have set a time bomb ticking in his body.

That brush with death seemed to make him withdrawn. Some students joked that he was "the strong silent type," which was not too far from the truth. Despite his reputation as a loner, he was sought out by other students. Ed held his own in his classes but shone in outside activities. He was president of the junior class, an officer in the military training unit, and a lead player in campus dramatic productions.

Fire was an ever-present danger in the lumber camps — during Murrow's time as well as today. But the use of steam, produced by wood-burning boilers, for the logging locomotives and donkey engines added to the hazards. Fire control methods were crude, and the lumbermen were sometimes careless.

Student leader

In the summer between his junior and senior year, instead of working in the logging camps, he attended the U.S. Army's reserve officer training camp. The military life held an allure for Murrow. He enjoyed the marching, the discipline, and the feeling of command. He returned to campus as a cadet colonel, the top student in ROTC. Then he was elected president of the student body.

His life was about to take a sudden and surprising turn. As president of the Washington State College student body, Ed went to the convention of the National Student Federation of America (NSFA) at Stanford University that senior year.

Ordinarily, a student from a cow college would have been just another face in the crowd next to representatives from the big universities. But that year, things were different.

The publisher of the *Los Angeles Times* had promised to make a $30,000 donation if he could be convinced that students were able to talk about serious problems. Eager for that prize, a group of student leaders who had experienced Ed Murrow's skill in earlier debates easily persuaded him to make a keynote speech.

Murrow called for students to expand their horizons beyond "fraternities, football and fun" and to pay attention to world events. The delegates were first spellbound and then wildly enthusiastic.

Murrow for president

The convention decided that Ed Murrow was the man needed to head the national organization as president. Back in Pullman, the students and faculty of Washington State College celebrated. Their president had brought much honor to the small college.

But for Murrow, it was a victory that left him puzzled. As NSFA president, he had won a job that required him to go to New York but that paid no salary. It would pay expenses if he could raise the necessary money from donations.

Students from the East assured him that they could find some place for him to stay. They didn't suggest what he would eat.

"Ed made the handsomest presence of anybody I'd ever seen. And the speech, it had such a polished quality, not a bit theatrical, but he was so poised. He was so confident and mature. I was just enormously impressed."

Justice Lewis Powell of the U.S. Supreme Court, recalling the 1930 student convention

Until the 1929 stock market crash, New York's downtown financial district was the center of world-wide action. By 1930, the stock market boom was over, but much of the excitement had moved uptown, where the new craze, radio, was providing a lift to both the nation's spirit and its economy.

Murrow was unimpressed by his first exposure to television. This TV set from 1950, one of the more expensive models and a big improvement over the ones he first saw, reveals why many broadcasters joked that TV was nothing but radio with pictures.

Changing world

When Ed Murrow left Pullman, he stepped into a world staggered by the stock market crash of 1929 and entering the Great Depression. Families were being forced off their farms. Great companies were going out of business. Men who had worked for decades were standing in bread lines.

Other things had been changing too while Murrow was going to school. Radio was coming into its own. NBC had gone on the air. CBS had been bought by William S. Paley, Ed's future boss. The world saw its first "talkie" — a feature film with sound. The first all-electronic TV set had been demonstrated. Sixty-five nations had signed a treaty outlawing war, and Mickey Mouse was born in Walt Disney's studio.

In the face of hard times, the "old Murrow luck" seemed to be holding. With $40 in his pocket, a cheap store-bought suit, and a head full of ideas, he was on his way to New York, the richest and most exciting city in the world.

What Ed found was a crowded, one-room, basement office in the low-rent district of Manhattan. There were battered desks, hand-me-down chairs, and a cot. It would do as a place to sleep for a few weeks.

Off to Europe

His main job was to find students who could afford to pay their way to Europe to attend an international conference of students and to take a tour sponsored by the National Student Federation of America. He got free passage in exchange for organizing the group. He shared a tiny cabin with his friend Lewis Powell (whom he'd nicknamed "Judge," almost as if he could guess the future — for Powell became a justice of the U.S. Supreme Court).

When he arrived at the conference, he made a speech calling for permission for German students to join the international organization. He argued that these young Germans could not be held responsible for starting or losing the world war of their elders. But the members of the organization refused to allow the Germans to enter, despite their enthusiasm for Murrow himself.

Besides attending the student conference, Ed explored parts of England, Holland, Belgium, Germany, and France. Wherever he went, he seemed to make new friends.

Return to New York

Back in New York, Murrow worked hard to bring success to the student federation. He increased the membership and solicited donations for the nearly empty treasury.

But the NSFA convention in Atlanta, Georgia, was going to be a special problem. The South was strictly segregated in those days; blacks were allowed in the big hotels only as servants. But the NSFA constitution demanded nondiscrimination. Both black and white students had to be allowed to attend the final banquet.

Ed had a plan. He asked *The New York Times* to assign a reporter to the convention and to be sure that the reporter was from the South.

Next he told the hotel managers that they had to serve all the delegates from all the colleges, as required by the federation's constitution. The hotel was eager for business and didn't question the list of guests, some of whom were from black colleges right in Atlanta.

Passing the plates

When the black guests started to arrive, the hotel objected. Ed pointed to the contract. He also noted that an important reporter from *The New York Times*, who was also a southern gentleman, was present. It would look terrible if the convention had to break up because the hotel went back on its word.

The hotel agreed to let blacks and whites sit together in meetings but refused to serve black students at the banquet. They would not have to, Murrow assured them. The black students would only sit in the banquet rooms with whites, just as they had in earlier meetings.

Ed had organized committees of charming and ladylike young white women to act as hostesses. Most of them were from southern colleges. When it was time for dinner to be served, the women took the plates from the waiters and quietly passed them to the black students. No southern gentleman would insult a lady by objecting.

It was the first integrated convention of a major organization held in Atlanta and the last for some time, but it was remembered for many years.

A venture into radio

In New York, up the street from the student federation headquarters, in a much better neighborhood, stood the CBS radio studios. It was a young network. A few years earlier, it had been taken over by a vigorous new owner, William S. Paley — a man not yet thirty years old.

Paley wanted famous people to appear on CBS. It was a situation tailor-made for Ed Murrow and the National Student Federation of America, with its international contacts with scientists and scholars. Murrow persuaded CBS that his organization could schedule persons of worldwide fame.

Paley mentioned Albert Einstein, the best-known scientist of the day. Later, when Ed actually produced Einstein for a shipboard interview during the scientist's visit to the United States, the network was impressed. It gave the federation regularly scheduled airtime for "University of the Air" features. Ed often appeared on these to introduce guests.

William S. Paley, who became both Murrow's boss and lifetime friend, owned the CBS network. He is portrayed here just about the time Murrow joined the CBS staff. Paley proved to be one of the most foresighted pioneers in broadcasting.

Newsreel

Things seemed to go right for Ed Murrow. He still called it "luck" but he worked hard at it. His initiative led to three new developments. He came to the attention of the Institute of International Education. He became a familiar figure around CBS, and he made friendships among writers, scientists, political leaders, and scholars.

If we watched a newsreel from these years, we would see Franklin D. Roosevelt become president of the United States. We would see Adolf Hitler become chancellor of Germany. The Empire State Building in New York would be opened as the world's tallest building, and RCA would put a TV station — one of the first — at its top.

That's what was happening as Ed went to work at the Institute of International Education. Its purpose was to arrange for foreign students and scholars to visit U.S. campuses as guests and to provide opportunities for their U.S. counterparts to study abroad.

This Nazi SS arm band displays the swastika. One of the oldest and most universal symbols, it appeared in ancient Egypt and Greece and on emblems used by natives of North and South America. Originally a sun sign, a benign symbol of good luck and well-being, the swastika became the symbol of the Nazis. In Hitler's hands, it unlocked primitive impulses of aggression and hate.

Scholars flee Nazis

Murrow made yearly trips to England and Europe. In Germany, he saw Hitler's storm troopers spread terror in the streets until they brought the entire nation under their control.

Hitler had risen to power with a vision of the supposed superiority of the German people and a hatred and persecution of minorities, such as Jews, Gypsies, homosexuals, Communists, and of anyone who sympathized with these people. Hitler's policies were driving many outstanding scholars out of Germany, including professors who had ideas unpopular with Nazis. Purges also took place in other countries with Nazi sympathizers.

Ed's work put him in touch with some of these great thinkers. For some of them, he was able to find places in U.S. colleges or universities, at least for a few months. For others, he found sponsors.

He always felt that it was he who gained most from the experience. This parade of professors, among whom he made lifetime friends, taught him about ideas that he had barely glimpsed as a student. He called this time in his life a "revolving seminar."

Woman on the train

Ed continued to work with the student federation, visiting campuses, giving speeches, and attending conventions. By now he was known as an expert on international affairs.

On a Christmas trip in 1932, he stopped to see his relatives at Polecat Creek, his first visit since childhood. As he boarded the train at Greensboro, North Carolina, to travel on to the NSFA convention in New Orleans, he noticed an extraordinarily pretty young woman sitting with a group of college women, some of whom he knew. They too were on their way to New Orleans.

She was twenty-one-year-old Janet Brewster, leader of the student government at Mount Holyoke College in Massachusetts.

"The chemistry was immediate," she told one of Ed's biographers. During the five days of the convention, when Murrow wasn't attending meetings or giving talks, he spent his time with Janet.

They rode back north on the train together as far as Nashville, and by the time they parted, they knew their lives had changed. After a long-distance courtship, Ed Murrow and Janet Brewster were married in the fall of 1934.

Then a new role opened up for Murrow, one he had not imagined for himself before.

Ed Murrow and Janet Huntington Brewster were married in October 1934. She was from an old New England family that traced its lineage back to the Mayflower *and the Pilgrims.*

Radio calls

When a new job was created at the CBS network, it was natural that Ed would apply for it. At the age of twenty-seven, Murrow became the director of talks and education for this national radio network.

For several years, Ed had worked long hours without a break. He wasn't very good at relaxing. This time, however, he was determined to show his new bride Europe. So before reporting for work at CBS, he and Janet set sail across the Atlantic.

They worked their way across as recreation directors, so it wasn't a total vacation. Ed also spent many hours with his high-powered contacts from the educational world. They would be important to him in his new job. Janet was astonished at the people her new husband knew.

Before joining CBS, Ed kept his promise to take Janet to Europe. Transatlantic travel in those days was by ocean liner. Ed and Janet, still short of money, worked their way across organizing bingo and other games on a Dutch liner similar to this ship. Janet discovered that there was no such thing as relaxing on a trip with Ed.

When Edward R. Murrow returned to take up his new duties at CBS headquarters in New York, Paley, owner and president of the network, was also impressed. He wrote a memo to his assistant saying, "Mr. Murrow might be the best one . . . for all our international broadcasting."

Early radio news

When Ed joined CBS, radio was much different than it is today. Radio seldom gave firsthand reports. The networks usually broadcast two or three five-minute news summaries each day, usually using short versions of stories reported by newspapers. If there was a big story breaking, radio networks would scramble to get a newspaper reporter or a public official to talk about it on the air.

The big programs, which were mostly entertainment shows, were created by advertising agencies, which bought the time from the radio stations. Unsponsored periods were filled with music or talk, many times just a performer playing solo piano.

Networks tried to get leading figures in the news to give talks about their views. One of Ed's jobs was to get important people to speak. He did well at it.

Fateful decision

But in Europe, CBS felt that it wasn't getting good program material. It was decided to send Ed overseas to its headquarters in London.

Even though Europe was in turmoil, with Benito Mussolini's Fascists running Italy, Hitler and the Nazis controlling Germany, and the threat of revolution elsewhere, CBS did not expect Murrow to provide news coverage. Ed was expected to arrange such things as broadcasts from grape harvests and dog and horse shows, readings by famous actors, and concerts by children's choirs.

Murrow was in Warsaw, Poland, arranging just such a broadcast when he received a call from Vienna. His caller was William L. Shirer, a reporter whom Ed had recently hired.

The Nazi army was marching into Austria, Shirer said, and Hitler was on his way to the capital of that country, Vienna. Nazis had seized the radio stations, the shortwave transmitters, and the telephone system. There was no way Shirer could get the invasion story, the biggest of his career, out to the people of the United States.

Murrow told Shirer to leave immediately for London, where he would be able to broadcast an uncensored report. Ed himself decided to go to Vienna to cover the story while Shirer was away. Within thirty-six hours, the world and Edward R. Murrow's life would change completely.

Airplanes and streetcars

Murrow was stuck in Poland. There were no flights from Warsaw to Vienna. He went to Berlin, Germany, but still no flights were available.

Imagine a time before jets, when air travel was unusual. Regular flights were infrequent and planes were slow, often grounded by bad weather.

But Ed Murrow was not a man easily stopped. He found a pilot and an airliner, rented it for $1,250, and flew to Vienna as the only passenger. His next problem was how to get into the city itself. With the whole nation going wild at the Nazi conquest, taxicabs had disappeared.

Murrow hopped a streetcar.

In New York, CBS president Bill Paley recognized the historic importance of the story. He ordered his network to do a special broadcast with reports from the major capitals of Europe giving reactions to Hitler's takeover of neighboring Austria.

That had never been done before. Paley himself had been cut off as he tried to talk to a broadcaster in Vienna. With the Nazis in control of key communication links, it looked almost impossible.

The *Anschluss*

Murrow and Shirer scrambled to find ways to get the broadcasts across the ocean to New York and to find reporters to tell the story. What's done every day now was a major effort then.

Vienna was filled with hundreds of German soldiers. Every major building had armed guards stationed at the doorway. The Austrian state radio station, where a Nazi censor was on duty, was especially well guarded.

Nazi Germany had taken over its neighbor, Austria, in what Hitler called the *Anschluss*, the joining of two nations. The capital's streets were filled with Nazi party members shouting "Ein Reich, ein Volk, ein Führer!" ("One nation, one people, one leader!").

Hitler was on his way to Vienna.

It was the biggest news story of the time. Those who understood what was happening knew it would change lives everywhere. The way it was handled could make or break CBS News.

Ed Murrow's years of building contacts and his powers of persuasion paid off. He found reporters who could speak from the European capitals, and he issued instructions on how the broadcasts could be sent to the United States. Although the Nazis had turned down both Bill Paley and William L. Shirer, Ed convinced the authorities that he should broadcast the news of their conquest.

At eight o'clock Eastern Standard Time on Sunday night, March 13, 1938, the United States heard its first "world news roundup," with reports from London, Paris, and Berlin. The reporter in Rome couldn't get his signal through to New York, so his story was phoned to London and read aloud for broadcast.

"This is Edward Murrow"

Also for the first time, radio listeners heard a calm, clear voice that seemed to take them right to the scene of the news saying:

"This is Edward Murrow speaking from Vienna. . . . Many people are in [a] holiday mood; they lift the right arm a little higher [in the Nazi salute] here than in Berlin and the 'Heil Hitler' is said a little more loudly. . . . Young storm troopers are riding about the streets, riding about in trucks and vehicles of all sorts, singing and tossing oranges out to the crowd.

"Nearly every principal building has its armed guard, including the one from which I am speaking. There are still huge crowds along the Ringstrasse. . . . There's a certain air of expectancy about the city, everyone waiting and wondering where and at what time Herr Hitler will arrive."

He said only what he knew would not cause the censor to cut him off the air, yet would give listeners a picture of a city under armed occupation.

It was 8:30 P.M. in New York, 1:30 A.M. in London, and 2:30 A.M. in Vienna by the time the roundup was completed. It started a pattern of long days and sleepless nights for Murrow.

Hitler returned in triumph to his native Austrian soil, beginning a long march of conquest that set the world aflame. The mobs in Linz, Austria, pushed forward in a frenzy to greet him.

107949

"He was fearless, strong-willed, and honor-bound by his conviction. It all came across in his wartime broadcasts. He radiated truth and concern. And America recognized and reacted to it."

*William S. Paley,
CBS chairman of the board*

A new kind of radio

This new kind of broadcast — instant reports from different places, an eyewitness story told the way people speak — was an immediate success. From then on, it was the way the best radio news was handled.

The next night, there was another news roundup and Murrow again reported from Vienna. Then he left Vienna on the very plane that brought him to the city. It was now overflowing with people fleeing the Nazis. As soon as he landed in England, in the small hours of the morning, he went directly to the BBC studios to relay the story back to the United States, uncensored.

He said he would "like to . . . forget the haunted look on the faces of . . . people trying to get away . . . the thud of hobnail boots and the crash of light tanks in the early hours of the morning. . . . I'd like to forget the sound of the smashing glass as the Jewish shop streets were raided; the hoots and jeers at those forced to scrub the sidewalk."

The United States was stunned by the Murrow style of reporting. CBS expected him to make more broadcasts — in addition to his other duties, of course. There were soon many chances to do so.

Appeasement

Hitler had moved troops into the Rhineland, the area of Germany that bordered its neighbors. He had outlawed opposing political parties, stripped the Jews of citizenship, and swallowed up Austria.

Although some voices in Europe and North America warned that Hitler's hunger for conquest would grow with each new success, nothing was done to stop him. Instead, British and French leaders of the time hoped to satisfy him by giving in to his demands. It was a policy called appeasement.

Hitler wanted an area of Czechoslovakia called the Sudetenland. British, French, and Italian leaders met with Hitler in 1938 in Munich, Germany, and agreed to let him take the Sudetenland. The Czechoslovakians weren't even allowed into the meeting when their nation was carved up. And their country was too small to prevent it. Neville Chamberlain, the British prime minister, told the world that "peace in our time" had been won by sacrificing the Czechs.

Opposite: The camera catches the intensity of Murrow's radio delivery. Despite his professionalism and the experience of thousands of broadcasts, he confessed that he never overcame his microphone and camera fright. Many great performers admit they suffer from the same trouble.

"In the birth of broadcast journalism, he had been present at the creation — indeed more than anyone else, was the creator."
Joseph E. Persico, from
Edward R. Murrow:
An American Original

"This is the last territorial claim I have to make in Europe, but it is the claim from which I will not recede and which, God willing, I will make good."
Adolf Hitler,
September 26, 1938

29

Thousands of children were sent out of London and other big cities to the countryside or even to the United States and Canada, where they would be safe from German aerial bombing. Janet Murrow helped find temporary homes for many of these displaced youngsters.

Sting of the nettle

During the so-called Munich crisis of 1938 — when the world seemed on the brink of war — Murrow made thirty-five broadcasts. Ed's great teacher, Ida Lou Anderson, listened constantly and wrote to him with her reactions. She suggested that he sign on by saying "THIS — is London," and that became his famous trademark, echoed by children on U.S. streets.

CBS had a strong policy against correspondents editorializing, which means telling the audience what it should think about events. But Murrow knew that his listeners in the United States needed more than raw facts. They needed to know the meaning of those facts.

He did this by finding some way to balance his reports. Chamberlain quoted Shakespeare by saying, "Out of this nettle, danger, we pluck this flower, safety." Murrow, calling up what he had learned under Anderson, knew the quote and commented in his broadcast, "The nettle is still there." That was in the fall of 1938.

It didn't take long for the world to again feel the nettle's sting. By spring, not satisfied with just the Sudetenland, Hitler gobbled up all of Czechoslovakia. And by late summer 1939, the Nazis had turned their attention to Poland.

August 31, 1939, was the last day of peace in Britain. Murrow told the United States how that felt:

"Tomorrow we shall see the children, the halt, the lame, and the blind going out of Britain's cities. . . . One million, three hundred thousand from London alone. Nine roads out of London and only one-way traffic. It's not going to be a very pleasant sight."

During the night, Germany invaded Poland. It was several days before Chamberlain announced that Britain was at war. He still hoped that he could deal with Hitler. But the British people knew the truth and waited patiently for the worst.

Blitzkrieg

Nazi forces struck Poland with the ferocity of attack dogs. Dive-bomber airplanes pounded cities, factories, roads, and military camps. Tanks and motorized troops sliced across the borders.

It was a new kind of combat that the Germans called *Blitzkrieg* — lightning war. Before three weeks had passed, Germany and the Soviet Union each had occupied half of Poland.

All of Britain was under a blackout; not the faintest light could be shown at night. Ed moved throughout London and the countryside, interviewing laborers, ambulance workers, air raid wardens, firefighters, bomb specialists, and powerful leaders. He wanted listeners to know just how it felt to wait for Hitler's bombers.

Subway stations, deep underground, were converted to air raid shelters where Londoners crowded together to catch up on their sleep while the Nazi Luftwaffe rained explosives on the city. Murrow never took refuge himself, but he frequently moved from one shelter to another to interview people for his broadcasts.

"Air raid warning sirens screamed through the quiet calm of this Sabbath morning. There were planes in the sky. Whose, we couldn't be sure."
Murrow in London, reporting the start of World War II on September 3, 1939

31

Sitzkrieg

France had also declared war on Germany, but there was an unholy calm. Almost no fighting took place as the British poured their troops into Europe and the French took up battle positions.

Along the border of France, the Germans hung signs saying, "We won't shoot at you if you don't shoot at us." In truth, Hitler's forces were taking advantage of the stalemate to build up their strength.

Some people made a grim joke of the situation and called it the *sitzkrieg* — the sitting war — or the phony war. The calm lasted more than six months.

But for people in the United States, things had improved that year. The Depression had lifted somewhat. There had been a successful World's Fair in New York where that new wonder, television, had been the hit of the show. The first helicopter had flown and scientists had experimented with splitting the atom.

But as 1939 ended on New Year's Eve, Ed told his listeners that the British were not sorry to see the old year go.

Hitler strikes again

The New Year did not bring better times to Britain. It was spring and Hitler was on the march. He invaded Norway and Denmark, aided by what was called a "fifth column," Nazi sympathizers inside the invaded countries who helped the Germans. These traitors stood ready to take over the government as soon as the German army arrived.

Neville Chamberlain, who had promised "peace in our time," resigned as British prime minister, a defeated and broken man, a symbol of appeasement. In his place, Winston Churchill, the old British lion, took over. To the people he said, "I have nothing to offer but blood, toil, tears, and sweat."

Ed Murrow's broadcast of May 10 told the story this way: "History has been made too fast over here today. . . . British unopposed landing in Iceland . . . Hitler's triple invasion . . . German air bombing of five nations . . . Chamberlain announced his resignation. . . . Churchill, who has held more political offices than any living man, is now prime minister. . . .

With Britain seemingly only days from defeat by the Germans, Winston Churchill took over as prime minister and came to symbolize the fighting spirit of the British. Murrow believed that Churchill's radio voice was the instrument that rallied the British Empire.

"For the last seven years he has sat in the House of Commons, a rather lonesome and often bellicose figure, voicing unheeded warnings of the rising tide of German military strength. . . . Winston Churchill, plump, bald, with massive round shoulders . . . The decisions reached by this new prime minister with his boyish grin and his puckish sense of humor may well determine the outcome of this war."

The German scythe

Later, Murrow recalled the disastrous events of May of 1940. "The British watched the German scythe cut through Holland, Belgium and northern France with a dazed feeling of unbelief. The channel ports were lost; the Belgians capitulated. We were told the British and French were falling back on Dunkirk." The *Wehrmacht,* as the German army was then called, forced 350 thousand Allied soldiers to the water's edge at Dunkirk, France, and threatened to wipe them out completely.

In one of the most heroic episodes of the war, ships and boats of every type — even private yachts and fishing boats, small and large — sailed to Dunkirk to take the retreating armies off the beach.

The ships and armies were under constant air attack, naval bombardment, cannon fire from land, and submarine attack at sea. This civilian and military rescue fleet took more than 338 thousand soldiers, including some 120 thousand French and Belgian troops, to safety in Britain.

But Britain was left almost unarmed. Trucks, guns, ammunition, and fuel had been left behind. The Royal Air Force was in tatters.

For some reason, Hitler failed to follow up his victory by invading Britain.

"Londoners are doing their best to preserve their sense of humor," Murrow told his listeners, "but I saw more grave, solemn faces today. . . . One woman standing in line waiting for a bus began to cry, very quietly. She didn't even bother to wipe the tears away."

Hitler's armies swept through France. Belgium surrendered. And Italy's Fascist leader, Mussolini, smelling a Nazi triumph, entered the war on Germany's side.

"It almost causes me pain to think that I should have been selected by Fate to deal the final blow. . . . A great empire will be destroyed. . . . I can see no reason why this war must go on."
Adolf Hitler's call for British surrender after Dunkirk

"We shall go on to the end. We shall fight in France, we shall fight on the seas and oceans, we shall fight on the beaches, in the fields, in the streets, in the hills. We shall never surrender."
Winston Churchill, after the removal from Dunkirk

"On this tenth day of June 1940, the hand that held the dagger has struck it into the back of its neighbor."
President Franklin D. Roosevelt's statement after Mussolini's declaration of war on France

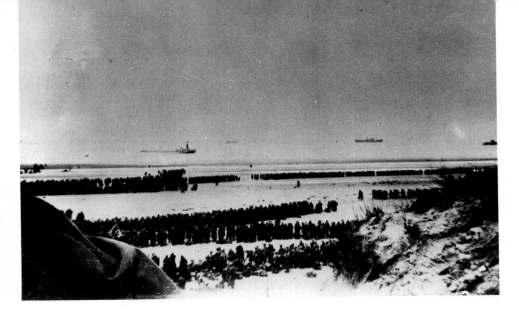

Thousands of Allied troops, forced against the sea in the Battle of Flanders, waited on the beaches near Dunkirk. Murrow went to Folkestone, on Britain's coast, to report on the exhausted, sunburned soldiers scrambling ashore and on the country's attempt to arm the coast for imminent German invasion with ancient guns hauled from museums.

Britain stands alone

With the European continent under Hitler's control, Britain waited for the death struggle to reach its shores.

The bleak mood was caught by Murrow: "For six days I've not heard a child's voice, and that's a strange feeling. No youngsters shouting their way home from school. . . . There just aren't any more children." They had been removed from London.

To the island came the governments-in-exile of the occupied countries — Belgium, Holland, Czechoslovakia, Norway, Poland, and others. Murrow put their leaders before the CBS microphones so that the public could hear directly what they had to say.

In the United States, public opinion about the war wavered. The ambassador to Great Britain, Joseph P. Kennedy, father of future president John F. Kennedy, believed that the German army was invincible and that the British lacked the will to win. The aviation hero, Charles A. Lindbergh, had seen the German *Luftwaffe* (air force) in action and believed it could not be beaten. He opposed U.S. help to the British.

Murrow, on the other hand, believed that the common people of Britain would make the difference — the clerks, the bricklayers, the bakers, butchers, and factory workers.

Their courage was soon tested.

The London Blitz

On the night of August 24, 1940, the Nazis sent one thousand planes to raid the London area. Murrow stood in Trafalgar Square, in the middle of downtown London, with an open microphone.

"The noise that you hear at this moment is the sound of the air raid siren. . . . People are walking along very quietly. We're just at the entrance of an air raid shelter." He let the microphone pick up the noise of distant explosions, the sound of anti-aircraft guns, the howl of sirens, and the calm footsteps of Londoners as they entered the shelter. More than thirty million listeners back in the United States were forming their own ideas about Britain's courage.

It was total war — war against civilians as well as soldiers, sailors, and airmen. Inflaming his people, Hitler promised to bomb British cities into dust. And he sent his planes out night after night.

Murrow talked to the poor, forced to crowd into public air raid shelters. "Germans believe Londoners . . . will rise up and demand a new government, one that will make peace with Germany. It's more probable that they'll rise up and murder a few German pilots who come down by parachute. . . . Most of them feel that even this underground existence is preferable to what they'd get under German domination."

A German bomber over England releases a stick of bombs. London was bombed night after night. Murrow noted the spirit of the inhabitants: "I've seen some horrible sights in this city during these days and nights, but not once have I heard man, woman or child suggest that Britain should throw in her hand."

"My hands shake so badly I can't read my own writing."

Murrow, in a letter to his brother during the Blitzkrieg

Hitler whipped his people into a frenzy with strident speeches. In the hands of Nazi propaganda experts, these speeches, broadcast on radio and seen in news-reels, became carefully crafted weapons of warfare.

"When an air raid is on [Murrow] has the habit of going up on the roof to see what is happening, or of driving around town in an open car to see what has been hit. That is a good way to get the news, but perhaps not the best way to make sure that you will go on getting it."

Elmer Davis,
war correspondent
in London

The rooftop

For fifty-seven consecutive nights, the Luftwaffe rained high explosives and fire bombs on London. Murrow told the story, sometimes broadcasting four or five times a night. His regular reports aired at 12:45 A.M. and 3:45 A.M. London time.

He carefully measured the distance from the flat where he and Janet lived to the broadcast studios — just five hundred paces — so he could find it in the deepest blackout. After struggling with CBS and the British Air Ministry, at last Murrow received permission to report live from the roof of Broadcasting House, the British Broadcasting Corporation's (BBC) headquarters in London.

On Saturday, September 21, audiences across the United States heard Murrow say, "I'm standing on a rooftop looking out over London. . . . Off to my left, far away in the distance, I can see just that faint red, angry snap of anti-aircraft bursts against the steel blue sky. . . . The lights are swinging over in this general direction now. You'll hear two explosions. There they are! . . . The plane's still very high!"

It had been a long, strange, and surprising road that brought him from Polecat Creek to this rooftop.

The time bomb

Although Murrow tried to disregard it, the danger was real. A 550-pound (248 kg) time bomb hit Broadcasting House, tearing through concrete floors. It had not exploded. When a bomb squad tried to remove the bomb, it went off, killing seven members of the BBC staff. Murrow was lucky. At the time, he was in the underground studio.

The CBS offices were hit three times but no one was hurt. The building where he and Janet lived was nearly empty now, everyone else having fled. Janet insisted on staying with him in London.

Ed seemed to carry the weight of the world on his shoulders. Deep creases appeared on his face. He grew thin and pale. The long days and nights, the constant strain were taking their toll. He suffered from permanent exhaustion and smoked constantly. He lived on coffee and nervous energy.

Still, he felt that he must tell the story of London's suffering so that people at home would realize that only Britain stood between Hitler and the United States.

As the year ended, German bombers still came, setting fire to historic London, sending its old towers crashing down, crushing its ancient walls. The city of Shakespeare and Jack the Ripper alike, of Dickens and of Sherlock Holmes was crumbling. "A thousand years of history and civilization are being smashed," Murrow wrote.

Draped in his raincoat, Edward R. Murrow became a familiar figure on London streets. In the background are All Souls Church and the BBC's Broadcasting House, where Ed made his many radio reports.

The man to see

Buried in work and over three thousand miles from home, it was impossible for Murrow to know what impact he was having in the United States. He was important to London, of course. Visiting celebrities, public figures, and people in business learned that he was the person from the States to see in England. He knew everyone, and all doors seemed to open for him.

But he could not imagine how the United States felt about him. Newspapers ran stories quoting entire broadcasts. He was often pictured in popular magazines. Newsreels showed him on the streets of London. The president listened to his broadcasts, so did cabinet officers and senators.

When he was ordered home, he got a surprise.

"Don't seem quite right, you gettin' paid all that money just for talkin' — especially since you don't sound any different than you did when you were talkin' and hangin' around the porch years ago."

Roscoe Murrow, to son Ed

A hero's welcome

Arriving in New York in the fall of 1941 for a three-month furlough, his first since he took up his overseas post, he was given a hero's welcome. Wherever he went, people crowded around him. CBS sponsored a dinner honoring him. More than one thousand celebrities rose to their feet, shouting and applauding wildly when he entered the room.

Archibald MacLeish, the respected U.S. poet, introduced Murrow as having "accomplished one of the great miracles of the world. . . . You destroyed . . . the superstition of distance and time. . . . You laid the dead of London at our doors and we knew that the dead were our dead."

Murrow's top boss, Bill Paley, called him "a poet of mankind and . . . a great reporter." The label stuck.

The banquet was broadcast throughout the United States, and radio listeners heard Murrow tell them, "Perhaps the final decision that will determine the course of human affairs will be made . . . along the banks of the Potomac," in their own nation's capital.

That was December 2, 1941 — five days before Pearl Harbor Day.

The president's secret

On Sunday, December 7, Janet and Ed Murrow were invited to the White House for supper, a rare chance for President Franklin Delano Roosevelt (FDR) to question the newsman and for Ed to learn FDR's views.

At dawn, the Japanese, without warning, struck the U.S. naval base in Hawaii, wiping out most of the Pacific fleet and plunging the United States into war.

Janet called Eleanor Roosevelt to ask whether the dinner would be canceled. "Come anyway. We all have to eat," replied the first lady.

But no one was surprised when the president's chair was empty at dinner that night. He had left word that Ed was to wait.

At last, after midnight, Murrow was brought in to see the president. Tired and gray-faced, Roosevelt still wanted to hear what the reporter had to say about the war in Europe. FDR, for his part, gave him a complete picture of the wreckage caused by the Japanese and the danger faced by the United States.

*Opposite: Franklin Delano
Roosevelt, thirty-second
president of the United
States and wartime leader
of the nation. His ideas
helped shape many post-
war policies. The only
president elected to four
terms, he died suddenly on
April 12, 1945, less than a
month before Germany
surrendered.*

Ed knew he had the biggest scoop of his life, information no other reporter and very few officials had. But he also knew he could not use it. The president had revealed his deepest thoughts to Ed, sharing secrets in a midnight talk.

National tour

Murrow then toured the country, signing autographs and telling his story to large crowds. His speeches earned handsome fees, but he gave most of the money to a fund for the families of Royal Air Force fliers.

Janet was also helping the children of Britain. She made her own tour of the United States to raise money for her work.

He and Janet could have stayed home and escaped danger. Instead, they went back to the war. "After much soul searching, [I] am convinced my duty is to go back to London," Murrow wrote in a telegram.

Air raid over Berlin

With the United States at war, Murrow's workload in Britain grew heavier. Among his tasks was to hire more CBS war correspondents. As usual, he was an expert at spotting talent, and he made an offer to Walter Cronkite, a young reporter working for United Press. But Cronkite turned Ed down, only to join CBS some years later, becoming a great star.

Murrow himself went to North Africa in the spring of 1943 to cover the fighting there. The tide of the war was beginning to turn.

Back in Britain, he flew with the Royal Air Force on a night raid over Germany in a Lancaster bomber, nicknamed a Lanc, and made a broadcast still remembered: "Last night some young men took me to Berlin."

He told about the briefing, the big bombers gathering into a fleet, the crossing of the English Channel, the battle with German fighter planes, the barrage of anti-aircraft fire, and then the target.

"Flares were sprouting all over the sky — reds and greens and yellows — and we were flying straight for the center of the fireworks. . . . A Lanc was caught by at least fourteen searchlight beams. . . . The lights seemed to be supporting [another Lanc]. . . . The German fighters were at him."

Orchestrated hell

"I began to see what was happening to Berlin. The clouds were gone, and the sticks of incendiaries from the preceding waves made the place look like a badly laid out city with the street lights on. The small incendiaries was going down like a fistful of white rice thrown on a piece of black velvet. . . . The four-thousand-pound high explosives were bursting below like great sunflowers gone mad. . . . The lights still held us. And I was very frightened. . . .

"I looked down, and the white fires had turned red. They were beginning to merge and spread, just like butter does on a hot plate. . . .

"All men would be brave if only they could leave their stomachs at home."

The British were repaying Germany for the Blitz many times over. "Berlin was a kind of orchestrated hell, a terrible symphony of light and flame," he concluded. It was among many combat missions he would fly, over the protests of his bosses.

After D-Day, the Allied landing on the European continent, Murrow flew over Holland with the greatest airborne operation of the war. Then he went to Paris to report on that city's liberation.

The Nazis had sown the wind; they reaped the whirlwind. By the end of 1942, the Allied forces had worked out a program to bomb Germany around the clock, with the U.S. Air Force flying daytime raids and the British bombing at night. Here, one of Berlin's largest railroad stations has been laid waste.

41

Murrow was so sickened by what he saw at Buchenwald that he felt his broadcast failed to convey the horror, but his words were quoted at length in newspapers throughout the Western world. "For most of it, I have no words. Dead men are plentiful in war, but the living dead, more than twenty thousand of them in one camp."

The evil-smelling horde

As Allied troops advanced into Germany, Edward R. Murrow followed. Entering the Nazi concentration camp at Buchenwald in April 1945, he was shocked and sickened:

"There surged around me an evil-smelling horde. Men and boys reached out to touch me; they were in rags and the remnants of uniforms. Death had already marked many of them. . . . In another part of the camp they showed me the children, hundreds of them. Some were only six. One rolled up his sleeve, showed me his number. It was tattooed on his arm. D-6030, it was. The others showed me their numbers; they will carry them till they die. . . .

"We proceeded to the small courtyard. . . . There were two rows of bodies stacked up like cordwood. They were thin and very white. . . . Some had been shot through the head, but they bled but little. All except two were naked."

It was a long broadcast. Many newspapers in the United States carried transcripts of it and the nation's people began to realize the extent of what the Nazis had done. By the end of World War II, the Nazis had murdered over twelve million people.

On V-E (Victory in Europe) Day, May 8, 1945, Murrow was back in London for a broadcast from Trafalgar Square, where he had reported air raids early in the war. He joined in the celebration, talking to the joyous crowds. But in the broadcast later that night, he told of walking up streets where friends had died and thinking about the people who had been killed in battle. "The price of victory has been high," he said. "The first task is to bury the dead and feed the living."

The news chief

The war in Europe was over, and perhaps Ed Murrow had seen too much of war. He was ready to go home.

Bill Paley and Murrow had grown very close during the war. Paley had served on General Dwight D. Eisenhower's staff, stationed in London, and had many chances to observe Ed in action.

"There was something special about Ed. And I wanted CBS to get the benefit of it," Paley said. He persuaded Ed to become director of public affairs — making him the head of the entire news operation.

Murrow proved to be a good executive. He brought new ideas into the organization and helped the company get ready for the growth of television. But he was not happy in management. Perhaps he missed being on the air, or perhaps the endless meetings and office politics made him restless. He was especially troubled at the stormy dismissal of his old friend, the first newsman he had hired and with whom he had worked throughout the war, William L. Shirer.

Before two years had passed, he was back on the air with the nightly radio news. Meanwhile, he had also teamed up with Fred Friendly, an energetic and talented young producer, to make a recording called *I Can Hear It Now*. This record told the history of the crucial years from 1933 to 1945 in the voices of famous people — Roosevelt, Churchill, Hitler, Will Rogers, Charles Lindbergh, Mussolini, Eisenhower, Harry S Truman, and others.

The record was such a hit that CBS decided to have Murrow and Friendly do a weekly radio program featuring important voices in the news. "Hear It Now" set the stage for Murrow and Friendly to enter television with "See It Now."

When they first teamed up, Edward R. Murrow was an internationally famous news star and Fred Friendly was an obscure, penniless radio producer. Yet they seemed to be a team from the start. Here they are seen in a control room working on their series of radio broadcasts, "Hear It Now."

"I can't get myself to fire anybody. I'm not the executive type."
Edward R. Murrow

Right: It's a good thing Ed was a glutton for work. Here he prepares for his program. This scene is typical of those repeated hour upon hour each week in order to get "See It Now" ready for live broadcast, warts and all — no videotape, no retakes, one chance to get it right. The program demanded split-second timing, coordination of a dozen elements, attention to a myriad of details, and the ability to improvise if something went wrong.

Above: During Murrow's time, live reports from outside the studio required a major technical effort. Today, mobile television units like this one routinely broadcast worldwide news events to viewers.

"There is no magic formula. . . . Our job is not to get between the story and the camera."

Murrow, from his book,
See It Now

"See It Now"

It was a new kind of television and a new experience for broadcasters and viewers alike. These were the days before videotape, so programs were extremely complicated. They had to be timed to the second; everything had to go right the first time because there was no second chance. Friendly became an expert man behind the scenes.

In some ways, it was the "old Murrow luck." He was there when radio news was growing up and now he was pioneering TV.

The camera liked him. He was handsome, he had a smile that lit up the screen, and he was beautifully dressed, a knack he brought back from England. He had a steady way of looking into the camera that made viewers feel he was right in the room with them. His voice, of course, was rich and confident. No one watching would suspect that he had always suffered from microphone fright and now had camera fright.

Audiences were astonished by that first program, Sunday, November 18, 1951. For the first time in human history, they saw the Atlantic and Pacific oceans, New York and San Francisco "live" on their TV screens at the same moment.

For the "Christmas in Korea" broadcast, Ed and his camera crews followed the troops right into the front lines. While today it's commonplace for TV to take audiences into the thick of action, Murrow set the early standard for bringing reality to the screen. One critic called the telecast "a visual poem, one of the finest programs ever seen on television."

Behind the scenes

It was a neat TV trick and many people talked about it the next day. But "See It Now" also brought Murrow and Friendly's audiences a taste of reality. Ed narrated the program from a working control room — something we see all the time these days, but a new idea then. It gave viewers the feeling of getting behind the scenes.

Murrow took his audience under the sea in a submarine. The program followed a pint of blood from the donor in the United States to the veins of a soldier fighting in the Korean War. The film team moved in with combat men and lived with them.

Ed's reputation for finding out the truth, then telling it straight, grew every week. When Lt. Milo Radulovich, a reserve officer in the U.S. Air Force, was asked to resign as a "security risk" because his father was accused of reading radical newspapers and his sister was accused of being interested in communism, "See It Now" investigated.

Radulovich was studying physics at the University of Michigan. He knew that if he were labeled a security risk no one would give him a job in his field. He was determined to fight against his accusers.

"His series of news documentaries, 'See it Now' . . . set the standard for all television documentaries on all networks."

The New York Times,
April 28, 1965

45

The people of Radulovich's hometown of Dexter, Michigan, were upset and signed petitions saying so. "The Air Force does not question my loyalty," the lieutenant said. "I certainly can't cut the blood tie nor do I wish to. . . . If I am being judged on my relatives, are my children going to be asked to denounce me? Are they going to be judged on what their father was labeled? Are they going to have to explain to their friends, et cetera, why their father's a security risk? I see absolutely that this is a chain reaction . . . that has no end . . . for anybody."

Programs stir protests

These were some of the very questions over which World War II had been fought — the efforts of the Nazis to control thought and to demand that children turn against their parents for political reasons.

Murrow called upon the Air Force to look anew at the balance between the issues of national security and human rights. A month later, the secretary of the Air Force appeared on "See It Now" to say that Radulovich had been cleared.

This and other programs in the series caused protests from people who wanted television reporters to ignore issues of human rights.

Senator Joseph McCarthy of Wisconsin. Murrow's courageous broadcast showed McCarthy hanging himself with a rope woven of his own words. Though many critics of then and now saw it as Murrow's finest hour, Ed realized what a tremendous weapon television was in a broadcaster's hands and how easily it could be abused.

Red Channels

During this period, many writers, actors, reporters, directors, musicians, and other workers in radio, TV, films, and advertising had lost their jobs because they had been named in *Red Channels*. This was a list of people accused of being Communists or sympathetic to communism. These people were also sometimes labeled "fellow travelers" or "Reds," after the red arm bands and flags the Communists used to identify themselves in the Russian Revolution. The list was put together by a group of "consultants" who charged business executives large fees to receive copies of it.

Red Channels was only one of the so-called blacklists that were being used in industry and government. These were part of a larger national fever called "the big Red Scare," a fever rooted in the fear that Communists would help the Soviet Union steal U.S. military secrets. And, indeed, spies were caught and punished.

The big Red Scare

Some politicians built their careers around red-baiting. One was Senator Joseph R. McCarthy, who attacked the State Department, the United States Information Agency, and even the U.S. Army. So powerful did he become that accusing someone of having communist sympathies is still often called "McCarthyism."

Joe McCarthy had a special advantage: The law protected him from being sued for anything he said in the Senate, and he headed a Senate subcommittee that he used to conduct investigations and hold hearings. He used these weapons to wage war on anyone he claimed was tainted with "un-American" ideas.

It was inevitable that Murrow and McCarthy would clash. The senator had given hints that he intended to use his senatorial power to attack the CBS network and certain reporters, perhaps Murrow himself.

Friendly and Murrow collected film of the senator's speeches and his committee hearings, of his television appearances and news interviews. They gathered parts of these into a half-hour documentary so that the senator's methods of bullying witnesses and opponents were obvious to the viewers.

No time to keep silent

Viewers saw McCarthy condemn himself out of his own mouth. At the end of the program, Murrow said:

"We will not walk in fear, one of another. . . . We are not descended from fearful men, not from men who feared to write, to speak, to associate and to defend causes which were for the moment unpopular. This is no time . . . to keep silent. . . .

"We proclaim ourselves, as indeed we are, the defenders of freedom — what's left of it — but we cannot defend freedom abroad by deserting it at home."

There was great tension in the control room. When the program signed off, telephone switchboards at TV stations all over the nation lit up. It was the greatest public reaction to a TV program up to that time.

Wherever Murrow went for the next few days, he received praise for the program. But the praise was not universal. Many members of the public supported McCarthy, and a number of advertisers complained to CBS, as did some TV station owners.

"The camera is a lie detector, and sooner or later you will know whether you're informed or you're not."

John Chancellor,
NBC news reporter

Ed and his son, Casey, roughhousing at the farm at Pawling, New York. Although Ed was a devoted father, work left him little time to spend with his son. He loved to teach Casey the outdoor skills he himself had learned as a boy.

McCarthy loses power

McCarthy broadcast a reply, using the half-hour time slot usually occupied by "See It Now." His answer did not impress the public, and some people said it made him look even worse.

The United States Senate eventually censured McCarthy and stripped him of his power. Many events, including his quarrel with the secretary of the Army, contributed to the senator's downfall, but Murrow's broadcast set the stage.

Questions raised in that broadcast continue to be asked today: How far may a broadcaster go in using the power of TV against a political figure? When is political power wielded in the name of patriotism being used lawlessly? Who is to decide on issues of loyalty and disloyalty?

The McCarthy program was televised in 1954. The senator died in 1957. Decades later, people are still arguing about Joe McCarthy.

Waves of crank telephone calls and hate mail washed into CBS headquarters, but Ed was worried only by the threats against his family. His son Casey, born during the war, was never left alone.

"Person to Person"

Ed's position at CBS was protected somewhat by his great popularity, especially since he was the host of another hit TV program — "Person to Person." He interviewed celebrities such as film stars Marilyn Monroe, Humphrey Bogart, and Elizabeth Taylor, the then Senator John F. Kennedy and his wife Jackie, and artist Salvador Dali. The show had many times the audience of "See It Now" and made Ed a familiar face in homes across the nation.

In the long run, changes in television ended Murrow's long stay at the top. An era of big-money TV programs with huge audiences began, including quiz shows such as "The $64,000 Question."

"See It Now," geared toward an audience interested in intellectual challenge, could not draw the same number of television viewers, those potential buyers of a sponsor's products. CBS began to question the value of its highly esteemed show with low numbers of viewers.

Political controversy continued to swirl around Murrow. His programs — on physicist J. Robert Oppenheimer (called the father of the atomic bomb), on apartheid in South Africa, on U.S. bombers based in England, on the issue of allowing supposedly Communist immigrants to enter the United States, and on the problems of small farmers competing against large agricultural businesses — all aroused protests. Sponsors hesitated to buy time for commercials and often withdrew their support from these programs. Yet these questions still haunt our public debate.

Smoking and cancer

Almost nine years before the U.S. surgeon general declared smoking a health hazard, Murrow tackled the subject of cigarettes and cancer in the spring of 1955 in a two-part series. Usually he was seen puffing away, smoke after smoke, but those nights he kept his cigarettes off camera. Perhaps Murrow knew that his own health was being undermined by smoking.

Tobacco companies spent large sums on advertising that the networks depended on for operating money. A show revealing the risks of smoking was a slap at the network's sponsors and posed a risk to its bank account.

In an atmosphere of declining revenues from his programs and rising political clamor about their content, Ed found himself with less time on the air. "See It Now" was reduced to an irregularly scheduled program. In 1959, "Person to Person" was dropped.

Paley's protection

Frank Stanton, who had started at CBS at the same time Murrow did, was now president of CBS and also Ed's boss. Even so, Ed continued to work directly with Paley, who was now the chairman of the board, skipping over Stanton's head. In the past, Ed and Stanton had disagreed about what television reporting should do, bring in viewers or explore controversy.

Murrow needed the protection his friendship with Paley gave him because he was under attack from many newspapers and broadcasters and politicians, as well as from powerful sponsors. Although Stanton kept quiet about Murrow's programs, he obviously thought they were harming the network.

Flags of Hawaii (upper) and Alaska (lower). A few congressmen objected to statehood for Alaska and Hawaii on thinly veiled racist grounds. They were concerned that, with the large numbers of Japanese and Chinese in Hawaii, communists from China and the USSR would influence the United States government. What should have been a well-balanced, noncontroversial show for Murrow became the excuse for his downfall.

"Why does Murrow have to save the world each week?"

Anonymous CBS executive

The last of "See It Now" came after a program that Murrow and Friendly thought would meet with general applause. For years, both the Democratic and Republican political parties had promised statehood to Alaska and Hawaii. "See It Now" tried to rekindle public interest in the subject, but a few conservative politicians claimed to fear "Communist influence" in the statehood movement.

Antistatehood forces were given rebuttal time on the program but demanded even more. While Ed felt he had presented a balanced program and these forces had already been given enough time, the CBS management agreed to give them more.

Paley's stomachache

Murrow was furious that his judgment had been questioned. He wrote to Bill Paley, saying that he could no longer do the program under such conditions.

No doubt Murrow expected Paley to smooth the matter over as he had so often in the past and to ask Ed to continue the program. Instead, in a meeting in 1958 with Murrow and Friendly that became legendary, Paley said simply, "I thought that you and Fred didn't want to do 'See It Now' any more."

Murrow and Friendly protested that the most honored show on television was being destroyed.

"I don't want this constant stomachache every time you do a controversial subject," Paley replied. He reminded Ed that he had given him editorial freedom and never censored his programs. Paley and Stanton had taken the political heat generated by Ed's programs while Murrow was the hero. The network had also picked up the slack occasionally when sponsors abandoned the show.

It was the end of twenty years of close friendship and preferred treatment for Ed Murrow. Nevertheless, he had established for himself and for subsequent news reporters the principles of independence for news broadcasts — principles that today still restrain sponsors from dominating broadcast news.

After seven years, "See It Now" had its last broadcast in July 1958 — a long run even for popular entertainment programs. The following year, Hawaii and Alaska were granted statehood.

After the last program, the television critic John Crosby called "See It Now" "television's most brilliant, most decorated, most imaginative, most courageous and most important program."

Quiz show scandals

Although Senator McCarthy's and the Red Scare's influence over the networks was fading, Congress wasn't through with the networks yet. The next uproar came from an unexpected quarter. It was discovered that producers of some big quiz shows were faking contests by coaching contestants to make their program more exciting.

Enormous prizes were involved — up to $100,000 was promised to the winner on one program — so the protests from losing contestants were loud and threatening. Politicians, sensing headlines, held congressional hearings that seemed to endanger the licenses of network-owned stations.

Among the many witnesses before the congressional committees was CBS President Frank Stanton, who admitted that the network had been caught off-base. There was a scramble to try to restore the prestige of CBS.

The big-money quiz shows proved to be based on lies. Above, emcee Jack Barry chalks up winnings for Charles Van Doren, the so-called "quiz-proof professor," on "Twenty-One." Van Doren was a respected scholar. His career was ruined when it was revealed that he had been given answers before the broadcast.

"Fred, when they say it's not the money, it's the money."
A former president of CBS News to Fred Friendly

"Itching pills"

Murrow had his own view of what was happening in network television and was appalled at the trivial nature of most shows. He told a broadcast news directors' meeting in October of 1958, "I am seized with an abiding fear regarding what [radio and television] are doing to our society, our culture and our heritage. . . . I would like television to produce some itching pills rather than this endless outpouring of tranquilizers."

He called upon the twenty or thirty biggest advertisers to use part of their advertising budgets for public affairs programs. "If we go on as we are, then history will take its revenge. . . . This instrument can teach, it can illuminate; yes, and it can even inspire. But it can do so only to the extent that humans are determined to use it to those ends. Otherwise it is merely wires and lights in a box."

The news directors applauded.

But the business side of the television industry was horrified. Stanton was critical of Ed's speech but, strangely enough, sounded much like Murrow himself when he spoke in public.

In the spring of 1959, Stanton promised a group of educators, "Next year the CBS Television Network is scheduling regular hour-long informational broadcasts once a month in prime evening time. We will report in depth on significant issues, events and personalities in the news. . . . We are determined to press the medium to its fullest development as an informational force as effectively and as fast as we can." He could have been describing "See It Now."

Murrow squeezed out

The CBS general manager offered Fred Friendly the job of executive producer of the new series, "CBS Reports." The offer did not include Edward R. Murrow or the Murrow-Friendly production unit, he was told. Ed could act as a news reporter on some of the programs but not on all of them, since "this would create problems."

Friendly couldn't believe what he was hearing. He told Murrow that he wanted to turn down the offer. "You ought to do it if they'll give you authority," Ed advised Friendly.

With that, Murrow and his wife took off on a leave of absence that was planned to last a full year and would take them completely around the world — the first major vacation they had ever had.

It proved to be a working vacation. Wherever they went, Ed renewed old friendships that extended across continents.

In many places, he was received with special honors. He did special interviews for "CBS Reports" as well as for his new TV show, "Small World," and for radio programs.

Front-page war

Into this hectic schedule came a bombshell from Stanton. On the front page of *The New York Times*, Stanton was quoted as saying that CBS would end program deceptions. He singled out those deceptions he said were practiced on "Person to Person" that tried to make rehearsed questions seem spontaneous.

Murrow shot back, also in a quote on the front page of *The New York Times*. According to Ed, Stanton had "revealed his ignorance of both news and the requirements of production. . . . My conscience is clear. His seems to be bothering him."

Bill Paley was alarmed to find the president of his beloved CBS exchanging transatlantic spitballs with his star news reporter. He sent a lawyer overseas to seek a peacemaking statement from Ed. Instead, Murrow felt Stanton should apologize.

Even though Ed continued to be seen and heard regularly on the air at home, he was far away and could not defend himself. The incident isolated him and cut him off from Bill Paley. Nor was he having much fun.

He didn't know how to enjoy a vacation. Ever since he'd been a small boy, he'd worked. He felt guilty when he wasn't working. Ed and Janet headed for home two months before his leave was scheduled to end.

It was not good news that greeted him upon his return in 1960. His sponsors had decided not to renew "Small World." "Person to Person" was at an end. CBS would not try to save either of them. Murrow would be only an occasional reporter on "CBS Reports."

"There were two Ed Murrows, you know. There was the journalist Murrow and the grease paint Murrow. When I pricked him for giving the 'Person to Person' questions out in advance . . . he did not like it."
Frank Stanton,
president of CBS

"This leave just isn't working out. I can neither sleep nor relax. The complete exhaustion is worse than when we left."
Edward R. Murrow, in a
letter from Switzerland
during his vacation

"Harvest of Shame"

The fight seemed to have gone out of him, but he had one last major contribution to make. He joined Fred Friendly and a young producer named David Lowe in creating a classic TV documentary that is still studied today as a work of art.

"Harvest of Shame" was shown the day after Thanksgiving in 1960, when most people in the United States were well stuffed with turkey and looking forward to Christmas. As the program opens, viewers see a dirt parking lot full of poorly dressed black men jamming themselves aboard an open truck as a crew boss yells, "Over here! Seventy cents a day. We pay more and longest hours."

Murrow describes the scene, "This is the way the humans who harvest the food for the best-fed people in the world get hired. One farmer looked at this and said, 'We used to own slaves. Now we just rent them.'"

CBS cameras follow the migrant workers as the workers moved with the seasons, picking oranges, cucumbers, beans, lettuce, peaches — blacks, Hispanics, poor whites. These people work, Murrow says, in the "sweat shops of the soil . . . forgotten people.

"The people you have seen have the strength to harvest your fruit and vegetables. They do not have the strength to influence legislation. Maybe we do. Good night and good luck."

He understood the subject and the people. He himself had learned to "hoe to the end of the row" as a poor farm kid.

Exile

The "good luck" sign-off was one he'd used since the nights of the London Blitz. Now it seemed to be almost a final goodbye.

When CBS announced plans to expand "CBS Reports" to a biweekly program, producer Fred Friendly proposed using Ed Murrow as the regular host. Paley rejected the idea.

After twenty-five years with CBS, by late 1960, Murrow was in exile, his career in ruins. His income was protected by a long-term contract, but he would be left to float around the newsroom like a ghost with little to do.

The urbane Edward R. Murrow didn't look a bit out of place standing in a farmer's field at the opening of "Harvest of Shame," the classic documentary about migrant workers that still delivers a powerful punch.

"[We] must hold a mirror behind the nation and the world. If the reflection shows racial intolerance, economic inequality, bigotry, unemployment or anything else, let the people see it. . . . The mirror must have no curves, and must be held with a steady hand."

Edward R. Murrow

In his distinguished career, nearly everyone associated with him had become a star. He had set new standards for radio journalism and had helped bring the television news documentary to maturity. He himself was still a great public figure, of course, but already he could see his light fading. He was becoming one of "Murrow's boys," absorbed into a crowd of broadcast reporters instead of remaining a star in his own right.

At this point, what he still thought of as the "old Murrow luck" took over again. The newly elected president of the United States, John F. Kennedy, called. He wanted Ed to head up the United States Information Agency.

It was a reprieve. He would still have important and useful work to do, work he could not live without.

Stanton and Paley did not discourage Murrow from leaving. Paley said, "You know there will always be a place for you at CBS if you want to stay." Stanton said nothing.

The network threw a big farewell party. Everyone was there, Fred Friendly reported — Paley and Stanton, as if nothing had happened. There was hardly a dry eye in the place.

In 1960, the first televised presidential debates pitted Richard M. Nixon against John F. Kennedy and ushered in the age of video politics. Nixon seemed hot, nervous, uncomfortable, and ill-prepared. Kennedy looked cool, confident, vigorous, clean-cut, and handsome. The camera loved him. The contrast is believed to have helped Kennedy win the election.

Morale rebounds

Aside from the president, Murrow was perhaps the best-known figure in the new administration. He headed an agency of twelve thousand people with the responsibility for telling the story of the United States around the world.

The agency had been badly mauled during the McCarthy era, and the morale of its people was at an all-time low. Murrow's appointment in 1961 turned the tide completely. "Suddenly we felt better about our mission and ourselves," wrote Joseph Persico, who was with the agency then. "If Murrow had found the USIA worthy of his gifts, then a new era had dawned."

Murrow set about the work of rebuilding the U.S. Information Agency. He wanted to make the USIA not just the voice of the U.S. government but a mirror of a complex, sensitive society. He toured the overseas information libraries and Voice of America stations, repairing much of the damage done to morale by McCarthy and his red-baiting.

Reunion

At the end of 1961, the Murrow boys staged a family reunion in Arizona, organized by Ed's brother Lacey. All the boys were successful. Lacey had retired as a U.S. Air Force general and then became an engineering consultant. Dewey had become a general contractor in Washington State. Mother Ethel came to the reunion but their father, Roscoe, had died in 1955 after a long illness.

But the trip had not been a good idea for their mother. She was in frail health and, on the flight back home, had to be met at the airport by an ambulance. She died soon after the reunion.

Then Murrow was struck down in midstride. While he was in the Middle East in 1962, he collapsed and had to be rushed home. After a brief attempt to recover at home, he entered Bethesda Naval Hospital.

Although he was eventually discharged, it was an illness from which he never fully recovered. The lurking lung disease went back to his mother's asthma, to the ordeal of the forest fire in his youth, to the cold and damp of wartime London, and the long hours of work without rest, all made worse by heavy smoking.

President John F. Kennedy greets the new director of the U.S. Information Agency. Unlike previous directors, Murrow often attended cabinet-level meetings. The president personally consulted him about information policy.

"[Our mission is] not to capture but to free men's minds."
Edward R. Murrow, to the USIA staff

"Under Ed Murrow the Voice of America became the voice, not of American self-righteousness, but of American democracy."
Arthur Schlesinger, Jr., in A Thousand Days: John F. Kennedy in the White House

Kennedy murdered

Within a year, doctors noted an enlarged spot on his left lung. They removed the lung in October 1963. Barely able to move, he was confined to his home in Pawling, New York, while he tried to recover. It was there, in bed, that he received news of President John F. Kennedy's assassination on November 22, 1963.

Murrow submitted his resignation as chief of the USIA the following month, due to ill health.

It was said of Murrow, as he left the USIA after almost three years, that he brought the agency "from the doghouse to the White House." There was no question that, as he had with almost everything he touched, he left it better than he found it.

As he departed, he reminded his fellow workers of their mission: "Communications systems are neutral. . . . They will broadcast truth or falsehood with equal facility." He urged them to continue to use truth as the touchstone of U.S. information policy, not to limit themselves to broadcasting only what would make the U.S. look good abroad.

Debate over that issue, among the many others that Murrow helped bring to our attention, is also very much alive today.

On November 22, 1963, President John F. Kennedy was assassinated while he was riding in a motorcade in Dallas, Texas. It is a picture that millions of people came to recognize with horror: Jackie, the first lady, in her pillbox hat; Gov. John Connally, straightening his tie; and the president, watching the gathering crowds. A few hours later, JFK was dead, Connally wounded, Jackie overwhelmed with grief.

"He has brought to all his endeavors the conviction that truth and personal integrity are the ultimate persuaders of men and nations."
President Lyndon B. Johnson, awarding the Presidential Medal of Freedom to Edward R. Murrow

Legacy of freedom

Ed retired to his beloved farm in upstate New York and remained there until his death two years later. Often Ed was found with a fishing pole — just as he was in the days when he was a child of Polecat Creek.

He had become world-famous, been given an honorary knighthood by Queen Elizabeth II, and been awarded the Presidential Medal of Freedom by the president of the United States. The day after Murrow's death from cancer on April 27, 1965, *The New York Times* spelled out his enduring legacy:

"Mr. Murrow achieved international distinction in broadcasting, first as a radio correspondent . . . and then as a pioneer television journalist. . . . His independence was reflected in doing what he thought had to be done and worrying later about the repercussions. . . . The fruits of his determination are shared today by newsmen at all networks; they enjoy a freedom and latitude not yet won by others working in the medium."

Some things have changed since that was written. Hundreds of newswomen have joined the newsmen; and some of them remember that Ed was among the first to open up the field to women correspondents. Other areas of broadcasting, like drama and variety entertainment, have also won much greater freedom — perhaps because broadcast news had shown the way.

Descendants of Murrow

Today, Ed Murrow could be said to have thousands of spiritual descendants all over the Western world. Reporters are found in nearly every television station and in major radio stations. Broadcast journalists are trained in professional schools of a kind unknown when Murrow studied in Pullman, Washington.

The technical problems he sweated over are routinely mastered today with radio and TV hookups that circle the globe with ease. When he saw the results of the first satellite hookup, however, he used his wit to issue a warning: "Now a lie can fly around the world before the truth can get its pants on."

Perhaps Ida Lou Anderson taught Ed the best answer to that with the *Meditations* of Marcus Aurelius:

"If it is not the right thing, don't do it; if it is not true, don't say it."

Opposite: In a pensive mood, Murrow is seen at his farm. He used the farm to put himself in touch with nature. He had become world-famous, but a hidden part of him still lived in the forests, mountains, and rivers he knew as a child.

Afterword

I write here of a man who, it seemed to me at the time I knew him, was the best man I had ever known. Nothing has happened since then to make me alter that judgment. Others, who knew him far better than I, shared that feeling. What lifted him above his fellows, I believe, was the one principle that seemed to light his life: the search for truth, his belief that freedom *depended* on people willing to search for truth, his single-mindedness about that.

In 1937, Murrow was CBS European director, and he went to Vienna to arrange for a program of Christmas music. He was still there when Austria fell into Hitler's embrace in March. His broadcasts from Vienna that month were his first. He had no formal news background or training. Those broadcasts were models of careful, accurate journalism. When people say that Ed Murrow was born to do what he did in life, that first month in Vienna may be taken in evidence.

By some miracle, it seems to me, the time and the place and the man came together. The birth of serious broadcast journalism can be said to be Ed Murrow's radio reports from Vienna in 1938.

I was nine or ten, and I remember my parents listening to the radio, waiting for his broadcasts from London during the war. "This is London. Early this morning, we heard the bombers going out. It was the sound of a giant factory in the sky. . . . It seemed to shake the old gray stone buildings in this bruised and battered city beside the Thames." The radio was on all the time, but when Edward R. Murrow reported from London, the kids at our house didn't talk, even if we didn't always listen.

At his death, he had been director of the United States Information Agency and an adviser to presidents and prime ministers. He was holder of fourteen honorary degrees and all the prizes of his profession.

But we don't remember him for his honors. We remember him, finally, for his deep and abiding belief that we could take it; that there was never any excuse for insulating the people from reality; that escapism was the eighth and deadliest sin; that the American people were wise beyond the comprehension of those who would trick us or delude us or tell us lies; that we were decent and responsible and mature and could be counted on every time if only we could be supplied our fair measure of the straight facts.

We don't remember him for his honors. We remember him for how he honored us.

Charles Kuralt
CBS News

For More Information . . .

Organizations

The following organizations may give you more information about radio and television journalism. When you write to them, tell them exactly what you want to know and include your name, address, and age. You can also contact your local radio and television stations. The larger stations often have tours of their studios, and some have facilities for watching a broadcast. Many will send a speaker to your class or club.

Education Department
CBS Broadcast Division*
51 West 52nd Street
New York, NY   10019

Museum of Broadcasting*
1 East 53rd Street
New York, NY   10022

Radio-Television News Directors
    Association — Canada
P.O. Box 235
Clarkston Station
Mississauga, Ontario
Canada L5J 3Y1

Radio-Television News Directors
    Association
1717 K Street NW, Suite 615
Washington, DC   20006

National Association of Broadcasters
1771 N Street NW
Washington, DC   20036

*You may be able to tour these organizations personally if you are visiting New York City. Write to them in advance to arrange a visit.

Books

The books listed below will give you more information about Edward R. Murrow and his times, and radio and television news broadcasting. Those marked with an asterisk (*) are written for an adult audience but younger readers may also enjoy them.

As It Happened. Paley (Doubleday)*
Broadcasting Careers for You. Hallstead (Lodestar)
Broadcasting for Beginners. Edmonds and Gebhardt (Henry Holt & Co.)
Careers with a Radio Station. Lerner (Lerner Publications)
A Day in the Life of a Television News Reporter. Jaspersohn (Little, Brown and Co.)
Due to Circumstances Beyond Our Control. Friendly (Random House)*
Hello, You're on the Air. Conford (Putnam Publishing Group)
In Search of Light. Murrow (Alfred A. Knopf)*
The Meditations. Marcus Aurelius (Bobbs-Merrill)*
The News Media. Wolverton and Wolverton (Franklin Watts)
News or Not? Facts and Feelings in the News Media. Weiss (E. P. Dutton)
On-the-Spot Reporting: Radio Records History. Gordon and Falk (Julian Messner)
See It Now. Murrow and Friendly (Simon and Schuster)*

Student Journalist and Broadcasting. Rider (Rosen Publishing Group)
Television in American Society. Cheney (Franklin Watts)
This is London. Murrow (Simon and Schuster)*
What Can She Be? A Newscaster. Goldreich (Lothrop, Lee & Shepard)
Your Future in Broadcasting. Rider (Rosen Publishing Group)

Audio and Video Resources

The following are actual Murrow radio and television programs. These are widely available through school audiovisual libraries and at some public libraries.

Recordings
Edward R. Murrow Reporting Live.
    Murrow (Bantam Audio)
I Can Hear It Now. Murrow and Friendly
    (Columbia Masterworks)

Films
Harvest of Shame. (CBS Films)
This is Edward R. Murrow. (CBS Films)

Glossary

Anschluss
    German word meaning "union." Adolf Hitler used this word to describe the Nazi occupation of neighboring Austria.

apartheid
    Literally means "apart-hood," a condition in which the races are kept apart through law. In the Republic of South Africa, apartheid promotes and maintains Whites' dominance over Blacks in every aspect of life.

appeasement
    As used in international politics since the 1930s, a diplomatic policy that consists of yielding to threats from possible enemies in the hope of avoiding war. Appeasement can sometimes allow enemies to violate treaties and take over territory.

barrage balloons
    Balloons anchored over a military target, such as a weapons factory or government buildings. Cables or nets are attached to the barrage balloons to entangle low-flying attacking airplanes.

bellicose
    Eager to fight or quarrel.

blacklist
    A list, usually secret, of persons or organizations that are supposed to be discriminated against. Blacklists have been used to keep individuals out of specific neighborhoods, schools, and clubs, as well as out of jobs. People have been blacklisted for religious, racial, political, and social reasons.

Blitzkrieg
    German word for "lightning war," an extremely fast strike into enemy territory, using tanks, attack airplanes, and motorized troops and guns. Hitler used these tactics in his rapid conquests of Poland and France early in World War II.

D-Day

The day on which a military attack or other operation is scheduled to take place. The term now specifically refers to June 6, 1944, the day Allied forces invaded western Europe during World War II.

depression

A period when business slows down, prices fall, and many people lose their jobs. The Great Depression of the 1930s was the most severe and widespread of all depressions. During this time, one out of four U.S. workers was out of a job. From 1929 to 1932, the total earnings of everyone in the country fell by half. Businesses collapsed, and farmers lost the land their families had owned for generations. When factories began producing weapons, uniforms, and other necessities for World War II, the general economy improved, helping end the Great Depression.

fascism

A system of government marked by a rigid one-party system that prohibits and often violently suppresses opposition. In fascism, the entire economic system of a country, including utilities, factories, and agriculture, is under the control of the government, usually led by a dictator. Fascism often encourages racism and the belief that one country's desires overrule any international considerations. It also glorifies military ideals. In 1922, Benito Mussolini began the Fascisti party in Italy. The term *fascist* now also applies to an individual who tries to dictate how others should live and what they should believe.

fifth column

Any group of people who aid the enemy from within their own territory. The term was first used by a general besieging a city with four columns, or formations, of rebel troops. He boasted that he had a "fifth column" within the city.

incendiary

Capable of causing fire. Incendiary bombs are specially designed to set fire to their intended targets.

McCarthyism

Red-baiting; accusing someone of disloyalty to his or her country or especially of being sympathetic toward communism. These accusations are usually made without proof and are based on little research or on unfair investigative techniques. The term *McCarthyism* was coined to describe Joseph R. McCarthy's activities during the early 1950s. Using his power as a U.S. senator, he badgered people, especially those in government and the arts, often with unfounded accusations of communism. His accusations caused many people to lose their jobs.

migrant worker

A worker who moves from place to place, following the agricultural crops and doing the unskilled labor of harvesting. Entire families, including small children, often move and work together. They do not have permanent jobs and usually do not have permanent homes. The homes they have, if a conscientious government does not intervene, are often without electricity, heat, and other necessities.

Nazi

A member of the National Socialist German Workers' party, which believed in absolute control of everything in life according to rules laid down by the party and its leaders. These rules dictated where people could work and what jobs they could hold, what they could read and what kinds of art could be shown in public. Like a private army, Nazis wore uniforms and used force to impose the party's rules. They believed in eliminating the Jews and other minority groups, at first by reducing them to slave laborers and, later, by killing them outright. Today a few people still try to advance Nazi goals and may call themselves Nazis, even though these ideas brought disaster to Germany and tragedy to the world.

newsreel

A short motion picture of news events, either preceding or following the main feature in a movie theater. Before television became popular, newsreels provided news documentaries for the general public.

night glasses

A pair of telescopes, each using two lenses. Light comes through the outer, or objective, lenses. This bends the light and focuses the image on the eyepiece lenses, which the viewer looks through. The lenses magnify the image so that the image appears larger and clearer than when seen with the naked eye.

red-baiting

Accusing a person or group of being communist, especially in an abrasive manner.

satellites

Compact radio stations revolving in space around the earth in order to remain in sight of antennas on the ground. They send or receive television pictures, radio signals, telephone conversations, computer data, and other useful messages. Because satellites can see so much of the earth at once, they are excellent for sending clear, accurate signals over long distances.

storm troopers

Members of the Nazi military force noted for brutality and violence. Brown-shirted storm troopers carried out Hitler's policy of racist attacks against Jews and other minority peoples, such as Gypsies, Poles, homosexuals, and officials who did not agree with the Nazi goals. They destroyed homes and businesses and arrested, brutalized, and murdered thousands of people across the German empire and Europe.

time zones

The twenty-four divisions of the earth, measured longitudinally. Clock time is measured by the progress of the sun across the sky, with 12 o'clock noon, standard time, being that moment when the sun is directly overhead. Because the earth turns, the sun does not appear overhead everywhere at the same moment. So we have divided the earth into a series of time zones to account for noon's progress from east to west around the earth. When it's 12 noon in London, it's 7 A.M. in New York. So when Ed Murrow wanted to do an 11 P.M. radio broadcast for New York, he had to wait until 4 A.M. London time to do it.

Wehrmacht

The army of Nazi Germany. The word means "armed forces." After World War I, Germany was forbidden by treaty to have a war-making army. So in 1935, when Hitler began a huge military buildup, he said it was simply for self-protection.

Chronology

1895 Guglielmo Marconi sends the first successful wireless signal, enabling discoveries that will sweep the world as radio and television. Thomas Edison and William Dickson, his assistant, invent the motion picture camera.

1906 United States scientist R. A. Fessenden publicly transmits human speech through radio waves.

1907 Lee De Forest establishes the world's first regularly broadcasting radio station atop the Parker Building in New York City.

1908 **April 25** — Edward R. Murrow is born (as Egbert Roscoe Murrow) at Polecat Creek, North Carolina.
De Forest makes historic broadcasts from the Eiffel Tower in Paris, France, drawing worldwide attention to radio.

1910 The first newsreels are shown.

1913 The Murrow family moves to Skagit County, Washington.

1920 Marconi opens the first public radio station in Britain, and the first Christmas program is broadcast from Germany.
The first regular commercial radio station in the United States, KDKA, begins broadcasting in Pittsburgh, Pennsylvania.
First broadcast of presidential election: Warren G. Harding versus James Cox.

1924 The number of radios in the United States reaches 2.5 million.

1925 Edward R. Murrow graduates from Edison High School.
Charles Jenkins demonstrates the first working television system.

1926 NBC goes on the air.
Murrow enters Washington State College in Pullman, Washington.

1927 Philo T. Farnsworth demonstrates the first all-electronic television system.
The CBS network starts.
The British Broadcasting Corporation (BBC) is chartered.

1928 William S. Paley takes over CBS.
The first regularly scheduled TV broadcasts start in Schenectady, New York.

1930 **January** — Ed goes to California to attend the convention of the National Student Federation of America and is elected its president.
June — Murrow graduates from Washington State College and moves to New York City.
He goes to an international student conference in Europe and arranges the federation's integrated banquet in Atlanta, the first of its kind there.

1932 Murrow becomes assistant director of the Institute of International Education.
He also meets Janet Brewster, his future wife.
RCA starts TV station in New York's Empire State Building.

1934 **October 27** — Edward R. Murrow and Janet Brewster marry.

1935	**September** — Murrow becomes director of talks and education at CBS.
1937	Murrow, now twenty-nine, becomes a one-man staff in Europe for CBS.
1938	Murrow's first broadcast as foreign correspondent describes Hitler's annexation of Austria.
1939	People in the United States get their first real look at TV at the New York World's Fair.
1940	**November** — The results of U.S. presidential elections are broadcast on television for the first time. Murrow describes the German bombing of London from a rooftop.
1941	Murrow returns from London for a furlough in the United States and attends a banquet honoring him. **December 7** — Japanese bomb Pearl Harbor. President Franklin D. Roosevelt's speech after Pearl Harbor is heard by seventy-nine percent of all homes in the United States. Television starts regular commercial broadcasting in the United States.
1943	Murrow accompanies bomber on raid over Berlin. He wins the first of five Peabody awards, which are considered the highest award in broadcasting. Murrow covers the fighting as the Axis Powers retreat from North Africa.
1944	Murrow reports on the liberation of Paris, France.
1945	Murrow broadcasts description of Buchenwald, the Nazi death camp. **November** — Murrow's son, Charles Casey, is born.
1946	Murrow becomes vice president of CBS public affairs and news division, starts a documentary unit, and strengthens its worldwide news operation.
1947	**September 29** — Murrow returns to news reporting and is heard nightly, except weekends, for the next twelve years. Murrow meets Fred Friendly and they begin work on a recording, *I Can Hear It Now: 1933-1945*, "a scrapbook for the ear."
1949	**January** — First televised presidential inauguration.
1950	Korean War breaks out, conducted under authority of the United Nations but using mostly U.S. forces. Murrow goes to Korea as a war correspondent. *Red Channels* is published and is used as a basis for blacklisting radio, television, and motion picture talent. Senator Joseph R. McCarthy accuses U.S. State Department of harboring Communists as employees. Murrow starts "Hear It Now" radio series.
1951	**November 18** — CBS begins broadcast of "See It Now" television series, produced by Murrow and Friendly.
1952	Murrow films "See It Now" segment, "Christmas in Korea."
1953	**October** — "See It Now" and Murrow cover the story of Lieutenant Milo

Radulovich, unfairly accused of being a security risk to the nation.

1954 **March 9** — Murrow's "See It Now" program on McCarthy is broadcast. Senator McCarthy is censured by the Senate.

1955 Murrow interviews J. Robert Oppenheimer, "father of the atomic bomb." Roscoe Murrow, Ed's father, dies.

1957 Senator Joseph R. McCarthy dies.

1958 Ed and Fred Friendly meet with CBS Chairman Bill Paley, who cancels "See It Now" after a seven-year run.
October — "Small World" premieres, with Murrow leading people from around the world in televised discussion.
Murrow denounces television as producing "tranquilizers" in a speech to the Radio-Television News Directors Association.

1959 Ed, Janet, and Casey Murrow leave for a trip around the world. Murrow's interview program, "Person to Person," is dropped.
Alaska admitted as forty-ninth state; Hawaii admitted as fiftieth state.
TV quiz-rigging scandals exposed; as a result, networks increase their public service effort.
"CBS Reports" begins.

1960 The Murrows return from vacation. Ed Murrow's documentary, "Harvest of Shame," is broadcast the day after Thanksgiving.
"Small World" is canceled.
Presidential candidates Richard M. Nixon and John F. Kennedy square off in the first of television's "great debates."

1961 Ethel Murrow, Ed's mother, dies.
Murrow leaves CBS to head the United States Information Agency.

1962 Murrow, reporting in the Middle East, collapses with illness.

1963 Doctors remove Ed's left lung because of cancer.

1964 **January** — Murrow resigns as head of the U.S. Information Agency.
September — President Lyndon B. Johnson awards Presidential Medal of Freedom to Murrow.
The U.S. surgeon general releases a report linking smoking to lung cancer.

1965 **April 27** — Murrow dies of cancer. Twelve hundred people attend Murrow's funeral, including many government officials and leaders from the world of journalism. His ashes are buried on his beloved farm in Pawling, New York.

Index